To Practice the Rhythms

节奏练习

To Practice the Rhythms

节奏练习

Shu Cai

树才

Translated by Ouyang Yu

译者：欧阳昱

PUNCHER & WATTMANN

© Shu Cai 2019

Cover image: Zhao Baokang

First published in 2019

Published by Puncher and Wattmann

PO Box 279

Waratah NSW 2298

Australia

http://www.puncherandwattmann.com

puncherandwattmann@bigpond.com

ISBN 9781925780192

NATIONAL
LIBRARY
OF AUSTRALIA

A catalogue record for this book is available from the National Library of Australia

Contents

三年

土地延伸着，转过
一道又一道弯，吐出
一座又一座村庄，最后
把寒冷的光，送给开口的坟墓。

我这把钝刀，在铁砧上，
敲，打，淬火……三年，
三年！奇迹发生了——
难道我还能从奇迹中返回？

Three Years

the land, extending itself, makes
one turn after another, spitting
village after village, till it gives
its cold light to the gaping grave.

I, a blunt knife, hammered on an anvil
have been hardened—for three years
three years! Till a miracle happens—
will I be able to return from it?

外面

那是谁，他拼命往外看？
那是谁，他拼命想看清？
但外面黑漆漆，
什么也看不见。

什么东西暗中指引我？
哪些事情值得问个究竟？

那是谁？他闭目内省，
而外面一日千里。
那是谁？他深入自己，
也被自己所深入。

但他拼命往外看。
但他拼命想看清。
他就这么活着，
又累，又努力……

Outside

who is this guy who is trying hard to look outside?
who is this guy who is trying hard to look, in order to see more clearly?
but it's so totally dark outside
nothing visible

what is it that is giving me guidance in secret?
what is it that is worth probing into?

who is this guy who, eyes closed, is looking into himself
while the world outside is advancing at such a fast pace?
who is this guy who, delving into himself
is being delved into by himself?

but he is trying hard to look outside
and he is trying hard, to see more clearly
that's the way he lives
exerting himself with weariness...

出门

你出门
然后回来
你出过远门
你抵达过一些地点
但我们总在家里
我们不想客死他乡
我们是怎样
从生活中回来的

在途中
你遇到过不少面孔
有几张钉进了记忆
除了免费的步行
你坐各式各样的车
大大小小的飞机
我们出远门都干了些什么
我们究竟是怎样
从旅行中回来的

你出过远门
从一座村庄
到另一座
走到哪里，哪里是家
但我们不是穷到家的穷人
我们出了门
总得回来
门外的世界黑洞洞
我们究竟是怎样
从生活中回来的

Going out

you go out on a journey
then you come back
you've travelled on a long journey
and have arrived at a number of places
although we always stay home
unwilling to die in a foreign land
how can we manage
to come back from life

on the road
you have met quite a few faces
a number of them nailed into your memory
apart from taking the journey on foot
you have travelled in all sorts of vehicles
and all sizes of planes
what did we do, travelling on a long journey?
how did we find our way back
from it?

you have travelled on a long journey
from one village
to another
it is your home wherever you arrive

but we are not so poor as not to have hearth and home

we've gone out on a journey

but we have to come back

the world outside remains pitch-dark

how can we manage to come back

from life?

灰铁皮

像灰铁皮一样无聊，像灰铁皮
这个男人，这场黄昏，这些吵得人
脑门发胀的知了，这从家庭到单位的
一去一回……

我醒了。
你挣到钱了。
他两手空空，伫立窗前。

一声吆喝使一平板车啤酒吮当吮当响。
一群灰麻雀从灰铁皮棚顶飞起
飞不了多高——
飞高了容易晕倒。
为一粒米快快跑！
为一粒米麻雀不知道天有多高——
不，麻雀不仰望。

等待太漫长，磨破了耐心。
打开的鸟笼目睹同样狭窄的低空。

像灰铁皮一样无用，像灰铁皮一样
趴着不动。麻雀不吱声。
夜轻易地吓退了胆小的人们。
跃过红砖墙头，民工的
身影闪入门帘。

白昼。夜。大地总有一只眼睁开。
这就足够。这就足够！
梦，然后生活……

The Grey Sheet Iron

as boring as the grey sheet iron and, like the sheet iron
the man, this dusk, these cicadas
that swelled my head with their noise and this commuting from my home
to my work unit…

I woke up
you've made money
he's empty-handed, standing by the window

a cry that caused the flatbed tricycle of beer bottles to clang
a group of sparrows that took flight from the sheet-iron-roofed shed
they didn't fly high—
high-flying leads to dizziness
run fast for a grain of rice!
and, for a grain of rice, the sparrows had no idea how high the heaven
     was—
no, but no sparrows ever looked up

the waiting was so long it had worn patience thin
and the opened birdcage a witness to the low skies, similarly narrow

as useless as the grey sheet iron, sprawling and unmoving
like the grey sheet iron. The sparrows making no sound

the night easily frightened the faint-hearted
leaping across the red-brick wall, the shadow
of a peasant worker entered, flashing, into the door-curtain

the day. The night. The land always keeps one eye open
enough. That's enough!
dreaming, then living...

日子

日子光长叶，不开花

时间的碎块，
日常生活的粉末，
灰尘和臭味，可触，可闻

日子光长叶，不开花

一些人被洪水卷走了
另一些上岸换鞋
就是没功夫看一眼周围

日子光长叶，不开花

赶路的脑袋上下错动
平板车上的家禽站都站不稳
有一棵树因缺氧而头疼

日子光长叶，不开花

造不完的大楼
数不清的灯
夜空的广告牌上月亮
被标上价出售

日子光长叶，不开花

时间的碎块
日常生活的粉末
这代人正把下一代往
悬崖上推……

悬崖上的日子光长叶
不开花

Days

days don't bloom; they just grow leaves

broken pieces of time
powders of ordinary lives
dust and foul smells, touchable, smellable

days don't bloom; they just grow leaves

some are swept away by the flood
others have changed their shoes on shore
they just don't have time to look around

days don't bloom; they just grow leaves

the hurrying heads popped up and down
the domestic fowl were unsteady on their feet, on the flatbed tricycle
a tree, for lack of oxygen, was having a headache

days don't bloom; they just grow leaves

buildings endless under construction
lamps countless

the moon on the billboards of the night sky

marked with a price for sale

days don't bloom; they just grow leaves

broken pieces of time

powders of ordinary lives

this generation pushing the next

to the edge of the cliff...

and, on the cliff, days don't bloom

they just grow leaves

死亡的献诗

1

同我宁静的黑暗，相反
整个大海像一朵莲花
因颤抖不止而闪闪发光
当一阵风吹来

这生命起伏的海面上
唯一的舞者是天空
风，她一刻不停地
坠入曾经之中
她来自天空的嘴唇

那是不可能的想象
在天边涌动
一直逼近思想者的脚边
像花瓣一样碎裂

2

这天空像一个圆
这大海像一个圆

生命围在虚线里面
一层层浪。远方的远方

这生命执意要去的地方
黑暗，静止，圆的中心
大地上的生者和死者
如同无数的鱼和沉船

死去的亲人也许
已抵达最单纯的梦幻
她躺着，转了一圈

而我，从内心到身体
同时挨近亲切的石头
在茫茫大海的圆桌边
智慧的人类不便再谈论什么

3
太阳的光明足够
让树木生长
让石头沉默
生长的，要在生长中沉默
沉默的，要在沉默中生长

临终的手触到了光
觉悟瞬间，光明是门
我扑向事物的母性
但你过早地
窥见了死亡

你得了致命伤
日子近于磨难
只有文字的盐
一遍遍，清洗伤口

日夜向上。但你
停留在半空中

4
死亡，这必然的风
我们沐浴其中
肉身的莲花，灵魂的莲花
春夏秋冬，四位神
调拨着风，弹奏着雨

死亡，这必然的运动
我们站在最基本的结局

哦语言像生存一样有限
直接的美愤怒着
走向灵魂的创造

你在大地上的脚印
为什么越陷越深
你在肩头上的重量
为什么越压越沉

因为从死者那儿
你采摘了未完成的死亡

5
你渴望美好地活着
更渴望美好地死去
白昼属于孩子
夜晚属于成年
瞧，你放下了仅有的书籍的武器
在自己的镜子前照了又照
一边说："一个相信谜的人，
自己也成为谜。"

但人类还有其它品种

暮色沉沉的海边，岩石之上
我呼吸着你的呼吸
你和我同时坐在风上
天边的花瓣在我们脚下碎裂
大海已抹平生死的界限

但死亡是最后一份厚礼

6
早夭的诗人具有灵芝的魔力
放弃：一种原理
因为我们只有一把尺子
时间的尺子

早夭的诗人是一支恐惧之水
回归纯洁的源头
通过在荒漠中的消失
重又登临雪山的峰顶

消失前的一瞬
你却折进精神的廊道深处
像宗教里发生的
不被证明

但你再次证明：只有悲剧
是宝藏

7
愚钝的理解力　永远
是问题的根本
我们跪下去，祈祷着：
更长寿些！
更快乐些！
更舒适些！
智慧和爱，对我们
是最可怕的疾病

我眼前摆着死者留下的
一行行密封的字
但我在洁白的空虚处
摸到了你的心跳

如果说这里面有手
那就是创造者的手
不堪孤独的手

8

悲痛是波澜

死亡却是药剂

我畅饮了噩耗

喉咙里呛出血

从活着的角度

我们看清楚局限

对于悲哀的人

迷醉是唯一的出路

对于沧桑的人

智慧是仅有的乐处

从死亡地点　回头

更艰难地　捉住

一个生者的要害

从死亡地点我不断回头

不断回头

以至看清去路

9

坐着　我和大海之间

有着可怕的距离
而你已在大海中央

大海里有鱼
日夜漂泊
会飞翔
大地上的黄昏
仍然散发着尘世的悲凉

死去的亲人
你用最深的爱指点了我：
思想，这最残忍的磨难

但一切又算得了什么呢
一切都是空的
空得溢出来
但我的迷妄还多么深
我热爱着大地上的万物

而它们致命的沉默
早已把我的心
带给更遥远的
事物。

An Offer of Poetry to Death

1

contrary to my tranquil

darkness, the ocean, as a whole, resembles a lotus-flower

shimmering as it keeps shivering

when the wind blows

across it, billowy with life

the only dancer is the sky

and the wind that keeps

falling onto her lips

that used to be there

it's the impossible imagination

that surges at the edge of the sky

approaching the foot of the thinker

breaking apart like petals

2

the sky is roundness

the ocean is roundness

life, encircled by a dotted line

wave after wave. Distance after distance

the place where life is bent on going
darkness, stillness, and the centre of the roundness
the living and the dead on the land
like countless fish and sunken ships

one's loved ones may
have reached the simplest dream
she lies, having turned around

and I, from my heart of hearts to my body
approach the intimate stone
around the round table of the vast ocean
intelligent mankind has ceased talking

3
the sun has sufficient light
to grow trees
and to keep the stones silent
the living will have to keep silence in growing
and the silent will have to grow in silence

the dying hand is touching the light
conscious of the instant, and, light being the door
I jump for the motherhood of things
but you have prematurely
glimpsed at death

you've been mortally wounded
days are close to suffering
except the salt of words
that clean the wound, again and again

days and nights upwards but you
stay suspended in mid-sky

4
death, the inevitable wind
in which we are bathing ourselves
the lotus-flower of a body, the lotus-flower of a soul
the four deities of spring, summer, autumn and winter
adjust the wind and play the rain

death, the inevitable movement
we stand at the basic conclusion
oh, language is as limited as existence
direct beauty, angry
is walking towards the creation of soul

why do your footsteps on the land
sink deeper?
why does the weight on your shoulders
grow heavier?

because you have plucked the unfinished death

from the dead

5

you long to live beautifully

and, even more, you long to die beautifully

days belong to the kids

as nights belong to the adults

look: you have put down the only weapon of books

looking again and again in the mirror of your self

as you say, 'One who believes in riddles

has himself turned into a riddle'

but mankind has other varieties

by the dusky sea and on the rocks

I breathe your breath

you and I, we both sit on the wind

as the petals, at the edge of the sky, break up at our feet

the ocean has smoothed having ironed out the line between life and death

but death is the final largesse

6

the poet, dead before his time, has the magic of a silver bullet

giving up: a principle

because all we have is a ruler
of times

the poet, dead before his time, is a branch of fearful water
that returns to its pure source
climbing once again to the peak of the snowy mountains
by way of its disappearance in the desert

and in the instant of that disappearance
you turn around and go into the depths of the corridor of spirit
like things that happen in religion
that can't be proved

although you prove once again that the only treasure
is tragedy

7

the slow-witted understanding always is the heart
of the matter
we kneel and pray:
let's live longer!
let's be happier!
let's be more comfortable!
intelligence and love are the most terrifying diseases
for us

lines of sealed words, by the dead
are laid in front of me
although I can touch your heart beatings
in the white spaces

if there is a hand
it is the hand of the creator
that can't stand the solitude

8
sadness is the wave
but death is the drug
I've drunken in the sad news
coughing blood

from the living angle
we clearly see the limitation
getting drunk is the only way out
for the saddened
and the only pleasure is intelligence
for one who has gone through the vicissitudes

turning one's head back   from the spot of death
the more difficult   to catch
the vital parts of the living

I keep turning my head back from the spot of death

turning it back

till I can clearly see the way ahead

9

sitting   I have a terrifying distance

between the ocean and I

and you already are in the middle of it

there are fish in the ocean

drifting day and night

that can fly

whereas the dusk on the land

still sends forth the chilling sadness of the dusty earth

my loved one, now dead

you instruct me with deepest love

that thought is the cruelest suffering

but what does it matter

when everything is empty

so empty that it overflows

but how profound my obsession is

for I love all the things on the land

and their lethal silence

has long taken my heart

to the things

more distant

犀牛

一匹犀牛从《圣经》上走过，
踩下了四个莲花蹄印。

我活到二十九岁：
这匹犀牛，这部《圣经》。

但这仍然不够！远远地，
一具肉身，在流动的死亡中，

在流动的鱼群中，又度过了
活生生的泡沫般的一天……

为了从虚无这块骨头煮出骨髓，
我的头颅必须是一口锅，

我的肉身必须是一堆干柴。
明晃晃的白昼，像一把大刀

又从我的后脑勺砍了个空。
我也习惯了自己的各种变形，

像尘埃的小天使们在光束中飞翔。
这正是肉身的一种本能。

一匹犀牛，一部《圣经》：
嚎叫的白昼，夜间的集体祈祷……

The Rhinoceros

a rhinoceros is walking over the Bible
leaving four lotus-flower marks

I am now 29
this rhinoceros and this copy of the Bible

but not enough! In the distance
this body of flesh, in the drifting death

and I have, in the drifting schools of fish, spent another
day of live foam…

to stew the bone of nihility till the bone marrow emerges
my head must be a pot

and my body of flesh must be a pile of dry wood
the bright day, like a broadsword

is hacking in vain at the back of my head
as I grow used to various transformations of my self

like tiny angels that fly, in the beams of light
an instinct of the fleshy body

a rhinoceros and a Bible

the screaming day and the night of collective prayers...

窥

1

九月啊，你松松手——
你一定要放过这个年轻人

这个人的命正悬在一根头发丝上
这个人还在跟自己过不去

他屡次求助于衰竭的死
他抓住这根头发丝不放

但是，九月啊，让他别太用劲
让他从泥土的方向摔向天空

不是由于鲁莽，或者绝望
而是由于超过极限的种种苦行……

他全心全意献出自己
他逼自己，上绝路，快马加鞭……

他那张被苍白扭歪的脸呵
蒙上了尘垢，残雪一样闪耀

相信命运之后，感悟神秘之后
九月啊，请察看这个年轻人的左手

他想改变生死分明的纹路
他已经弄乱了五脏六腑

他反复强调："我熬过了八月，
我怕熬不过九月了……"

他的命还不老，但他已在拼老命
他的寿数还在，但他每天窥见死

2
九月，我不能告诉你过多的细节。
关于一个极端的人，我只好哑口无言。

他也没能告诉我。他结巴得像块石头，
他掏自己的内，但他掏不出。

九月，他相信了"那个东西"！
为"它"而死，当然—值得。

不可能的谈心，持续了半夜。
我的这一端已不可能接通他的另一端。

他这么专注于造就自己，
他把命委托给另一条命。

真理的残酷，在他身上，噢
又一场雪冻死一根枯枝……

他究竟想干什么？谁也不可能
阻止他。众人任他飞奔。

他要是飞奔在天空中该多自由！
他要是真能弃绝尘世该多了不起！

他命令自己做那无法做到的……
他肉身的每一寸土地都在说—不……

九月啊，只有你能救助他—
不，只有他自己。只有他自己！

太高了，他几乎耗尽全部力气。
太难了，他居然乐于试一试。

九月啊，请注视奇迹出现的一瞬，
请将这瞬间暗暗显现给世人。

3
啊，我窥见了—九月的眼瞳
一个人万劫不变的厄运

在核桃树下，如同在石桌旁
谁又能窥见另一个灵魂的急转弯

我窥见他出现在另一条地平线上
他越走越小。这个点，只有光追踪它

他误入自己布设的陷阱了—
啊，他在自己的陷阱里苦苦挣扎

他忘了怎么解开自己打的绳结
他说："我只能往前冲，往前冲……

我不能退，我退就死了……"
誓言代替了遗言，我哑口无言

我哑口无言的脸竟收不住最后一缕微笑
向一个濒死的人我竟然抛出存在的话题

啊，我窥见了—救过我的九月之神
正在稻草堆里打盹

我也在打盹！让我摸一下他的脸
让我留给他这最后一缕微笑

这一切多么惊人啊！他
截短了自觉献身的尺子

他如果真的死了，他如果真的死了
九月，说明你在稻草堆里还不想睁开眼

如果他真的死了，这死本身便成奇迹
九月，你支撑这个悬在头发丝上的人吧

4

我走进这个地方，一个"窥"字抓住我——
我怎能抵得住这一暗示？我又怎么敢！

我坐着，我走动，我吃透这个"窥"字——
不，我窥视的姿势变化得还不够快

我来到一棵榆树下，窥见一只知了——
这短命的甲壳虫从夏天嚷到九月

我穿过一条街道，顺便买好蔬菜
活下去和怎么活，不全在一念之差

他就不同。不，他没有什么不同
我没能窥见他惟一持久的东西

不同于清浅的感伤，命该如此的人
又怎能及时窥见那条命？

麻烦事不断。他想让尾巴长出
他反复说："那东西是真的。"

我没有掉以轻心，我窥见了不少人
正口吐白沫，要告诉我我的命

每个人只相信他所深信的——
世间无天真。怜悯很远，远及天外

不能不死的在修理死
日日夜夜，他不离开他的打字机

他不离开，否则他的命要离开
九月，让他腾出身子，触摸少女

他不腾出身子，他只用眼睛瞟瞟
他瞟瞟就够，他足以窥见。

5
九月，请救援他，请放他一马——
他每天都窥见死，他生死未卜。

这不是一匹马，这是一个人呵——
死神窥见自己占了上风。

他枯坐的身子一挪动，
整个天空就会崩塌。

九月，他从指头上扳倒一个个日子。
病弱的鞭子，抽打他，又不许他喊疼。

他当然喊过，他大声喊过疼。
但公路两边的行人没有一个理他。

他躲起来。他秘密地向死的圣地进军，
十月可能会死在他的舌头底下。

他多么想撑过九月！
但是，九月啊，你清楚……他生死未卜。

十月即不死，即永远……
九月，一匹瘦马能否挤出你的窄门？

色、香、味俱全的乌托邦呵，
他跳上的贼船不允许他上岸！

"好了，让我给你讲一段轻松的寓言吧……"
他说—被苦水泡歪的嘴句句吐血。

Glimpses

1

ah, September, let go—
you must let go of this young man

whose life is hanging on a single hair
and who is still going against himself

on numerous occasions he seeks help from the failing death
grabbing hold of this hair

but, ah, September, don't let him exert himself
do let him throw himself into the sky from the direction of earth

not because of any recklessness or despair
but because of asceticism of all sorts exceeding the limit...

he's wholeheartedly offered himself
he's forcing himself, into a blind alley, at top speed...

ah, his face distorted by its paleness
covered in dust, shines like the remaining snow

ah, September, after you believe in fate and
intuit the mysteries, please examine the young man's left hand

for he wants to change the distinct veins of life and death
having disturbed the viscera

he keeps repeating: 'I've endured August
and am afraid I may not be able to endure September...'

he's not yet old but he's struggling with his ageing life
his days are not yet numbered but he gets glimpses of death daily

2
september, I can't give you too much detail
I have to remain mute about an extreme person

nor can he tell me anything, stammering like a stone
he is fetching, in vain, from his insides

in September, he believes 'that thing'!
but, of course, it's worth dying for 'it'

an impossible heart-to-heart talk lasted half the night
but this end of mine was not able to connect with that end of his

he's so focused on building himself

consigning his life to another life

oh, the cruel truth, in him

another snow has frozen a withered branch to death...

what on earth does he want to do? No one can

stop him. They all let him run flying

wouldn't it be such freedom if only he could run flying in the sky?

wouldn't it be wonderful if he could really abandon this dusty earth?

he orders himself to attempt the impossible...

every inch of his body says no...

ah, September, you are the only one who can save him—

no, he himself is the only one. He himself!

it's so high that he has almost exhausted himself

it's so hard that he's even happy to try

ah, September, please watch the moment of miracle

please secretly reveal the moment to the world

3

ah, I've glimpsed into—the pupils of September

the doom of someone who remains unchanging after so many disasters

under the walnut tree, like by the stone table

who can glimpse the sharp turn of another soul?

but I glimpsed him appearing on another horizon

as he becomes smaller, the dot that only light can follow, chasing

he has, by mistake, fallen into the trap he's laid for himself—

ah, he's struggling in it with bitterness

forgetting how to loosen the knot, tied up by himself

he said, 'All I can do is rush ahead, rushing ahead…

I can't retreat or I die…'

his vow replacing his last words, striking me dumb

my face, struck dumb, was unable to take back its last smile

as I threw a subject of survival to a dying person

ah, I've glimpsed—the Deity of September that has saved me

dozing in the hay

I, too, am dozing! Let me touch his face
let me keep this last smile for him

how astonishing all that is! He
has shortened the measurement of death by his own conscious hand

if he really died, and if he really died
September, it means you still do not want to open your eyes in the hay

if he really died, the death would become a miracle itself
September, support him who's hanging on a single hair

4
as I enter the place, the word 'glimpse' catches hold of me—
how can I resist the hint? How dare I?

I sit, I move and I attempt a thorough understanding of the word—
no, my posture of glimpsing does not change fast enough

I come to an elm and I glimpse a cicada—
this short-lived beetle has been howling till September

I cross a street and buy the vegetables along the way
the difference between how to keep living and how to live is but a mere
      thought

he's different. No. He's not really different
I haven't glimpsed the only thing that lasts of him

how can a man with a fate like that, different from the shallow
        sentimentality
glimpse the life in a timely manner?

endless troubles. He wants the tail to grow
he keeps saying, 'That is real'

I did not let down my guard for I have glimpsed quite a few
foaming at the mouth and wanting to tell me about my fate

each convinced of what he deeply believes in
no innocence exists. Compassion is so far it's beyond the sky

one, unable to die, is fixing death
day and night, he can't leave his typewriter

he doesn't leave or his life will leave
September, let him disengage himself, to touch the girl

he doesn't disengage himself; he only glimpses
the glimpsing is sufficient for him to see

5

september, please rescue him and give him a break—
he glimpses death daily, his life uncertain

this is not a horse, this is an individual—
death, the Deity, has glimpsed that he is having the upper hand

once his idly sitting body moves
the whole sky will collapse

in September, when he fells one day after another on his fingers
the sick whip lashes him, forbidding him to complain of pain

of course he did complain, loudly, of pain
but no passers-by on the road paid him any attention

he went into hiding and, in secret, he advanced towards the Mecca of death
October may die underneath his tongue

how he wishes to survive September!
but, ah, September, you know…that his life is uncertain

October means undying, it means everlasting…
September, can a thin horse squeeze itself out of your narrow door?

a utopia complete with colours, fragrances and tastes

but the ship of thieves he stowed away in does not allow him ashore!

'all right, let me tell you a light fable…'

he said—his mouth, distorted with bitter water, spits sentences of blood

汉字

一个汉字，
我盯着它。
它自己打开了，
连它最隐秘的部分，
也被我察觉。

一个汉字，
自己打开，
又自己闭合。
这中间的间歇，
花掉了我的一生。

The Chinese Characters

a Chinese character.
as I gaze at it
it opens itself
till I become aware of
its most secret parts.

a Chinese character
opens itself
and closes itself.
the interval
exhausts my entire life.

高烧

高烧煮了我整整三天
打针，吃药，受庸医的气
我这根瘦骨头，总算
没有被煮透

细菌性感冒。一夜之间
把我掀翻
一声声干咳的利剑
刺穿了我的腹背

这是个交叉传染的世界
好与坏一样多
高烧过后，是虚弱
干咳过后，是虚热

悬空的阳台。毯子蒙住
膝盖。脑子里一锅粥
我提前过起了
孤零零的老年人退休生活

病中心事越想越少
朋友也变得简单
数来数去，就那么几个
又该剪一剪生活的枝蔓了

High Fever

the high fever has been stewing me for three solid days
injections, medications, and getting upset with the quack
so that my thin bones manage to stay
unstewed through

a bacterial cold knocked me down
overnight
dry coughs, like swords
pierced my belly and my back

this is a world of cross infection
with as many goodnesses as bad
feebleness following the fever
and heat following the dry coughs

the balcony suspended. Knees covered
with a blanket. Head a pot of congee
ahead of time, I started living
the solitude of an old man in retirement

in my illness, I thought less and less
my friends had become simple

and, even though I kept counting, there were only such a few

once again, I have to prune the branches of life

某个人

某个人？可以是你，是我，是他。
某个人躲在某个名字下。
某个人喃喃低语，对风说话。
第一个某个人不知道自己叫什么。

某个人死了！脸过渡为面具。
有几种面具不能让妇女看见。
但在人类的厨房里，时间的
菜刀，需要死亡这块磨刀石。

某个人，见过面的，说过话的，
死了的，还未出生的……
某个人正迎面走来，
某个人已擦肩而过。

据说某个人生来清白，
据说柏拉图经历了苏格拉底之死，
通过他的嘴，死亡唾沫四溅，
通过他的笔，死者重返街道。

某个人，生于XXX,

死于XXX。

生死之间，夹着一小段生活。

而生活，是负债的过程。

死亡是中断。某个人继续……

Someone

someone? It could be you, could be I or it could be him.

someone hides beneath a name.

someone murmurs, talking to the wind.

the first someone does not know what his name is.

someone dies, his face transformed into a mask.

several masks not allowed for women to see.

but, in the kitchen of mankind, the knife

of time needs the grindstone of death.

someone, seen, spoken to

dead, or not yet born...

someone is coming towards me

and someone has just brushed past.

they say someone is born pure

they say Plato experienced the death of Socrates

through whose mouth death spits all over the place

and through whose pen death returns to the streets.

someone, born in such and such a year

and died in such and such a year

a small segment of life in between

and life, a process of becoming ridden with debt.

death is an interruption. Someone is continuing...

刀削面

安德路口，电线杆旁，
一个矮汉在削刀削面。

他的脖颈一伸一缩，
他的眼睛盯住刀片，

他的下巴一勾一勾，
他的右肘甩着来回，

面条条儿一蹦一跳，
赤条条地滚进大锅。

他从离下巴最近的那儿
削起，一刀一刀往上移，

再落下来，再一刀刀
往上移，麻利，娴熟，

客人们坐等着……

很快，手掌就托不住了。
矮汉趁机瞟了一眼周围，

顺便吐一口长气，调匀
呼吸，让刀片刮刮锅沿，

对剩下的面坨下手。

这时过来一位粗辫子丫头，
用大漏勺往锅里那么一搅，

捞满了面条，再往上一抖，
顺势就送进了一只大海碗，

一看不够，再添点儿，
然后，酱油、盐、醋……

最后撒一撮香菜。
得，您吃去吧！

出租司机正埋头扒拉。

这小面摊紧挨着建筑工地。
载重卡车开进去，又出来。

这儿的气氛热热闹闹，
这儿的灰尘一阵一阵。

红色夏利塞满了路口，
民工们吃饱了，歇着，

一面面小红旗悠悠地飘呀，
一碗刀削面足够顶一个下午。

The Knife-Sliced Noodles

at the intersection of Ande Road and by a lamppost
a short man is slicing noodles with a knife

his neck extending and contracting
and his eyes fixed on the blade of a knife

he keeps lifting his chin
as his right elbow moves back and forth

the noodles roll, bouncing and leaping
nakedly into the wok

he starts slicing from where it's closest
to the chin, moving upwards with each slice

before it falls, moving upwards again
with each slicing, in a neat and adept manner

while his clients sit waiting...

soon enough his hand can't hold it any longer
the short man, glancing around him

breathes out a long breath and, adjusting
his breath, he scrapes the edge of the wok with the blade of his knife

dealing a blow to the dough

when a girl, with thick pigtails, comes over
and stirs inside the wok with a huge strainer

scooping a full scoop of the noodles and, with an upward shake
delivering the whole thing into an ocean bowl along the way

when she sees that it's not enough, she puts in a bit more
with soy sauce, salt and vinegar...

before garnishing it with a pinch of parsley
here you go!

the cabdriver has his nose in it right now!

the noodle stand is close to the construction site
where the trucks come and go

raising much dust
in an atmosphere of heat and noise

the intersection crowded with the red Xialis

the peasant workers, having feasted, are resting up

the small red flags are fluttering

a bowl of knife-sliced noodles can last a whole afternoon

去九寨沟的路上

快，快，快，
中巴车开得贼快。

岷江一路相伴，
隆隆渐渐潺潺。

细腰，细腰……
电话线奔跑如妖。

庄稼，树木，
从车窗两侧急退。

爬，爬，爬，
爬上高原，是平的。

岷江坠下去，
在沟底冒白沫。

山脚看不见了。
山头近在眼前。

野草满目呵，
野花被风灌醉。

白云扬眉，是鹿，
白云伸腰，是狗。

白云，白云……
鞭响处羊群乱窜。

九寨沟太美了，
因为离城里远。

快，快，快，
中巴车好几次想翻。

司机说以前去成都，
每次都有伙伴

把车开进岷江，
把命送给鱼虾……

五天一趟来回，
辛苦，能赚钱！

旅客们困睡了，
他唱青藏高原。

On the Way to Jiuzhaigou

quick, quick, quick
the minibus is going so fucking fast

the Minjiang River keeping company all the way
rumbling and bubbling

a thin waist, another thin waist...
telephone lines are running like fairies

the crop, the trees
fast receding on either window of the bus

climbing, climbing, still climbing
onto the plateau, so plain

where the Minjiang River takes the plunge
turning into white foam at the bottom of the valley

the foot of the mountain is invisible
its head, though, is right under my eye

filling it with wild grasses
and wild flowers, intoxicated with the wind

the white clouds lifting their brows are deer

and, when they straighten themselves up, are dogs

white clouds, white clouds...

the sheep are running helter-skelter at the crack of a whip

so beautiful is Jiuzhaigou

because it's so far away from any cities

quick, quick, quick

the minibus, on several occasions, wants to overturn itself

according to the driver, each time he drove to Chengdu in the past

his companions would

drive their busses into the Minjiang River

feeding the fish and shrimps with their own lives...

a return trip costs five days

hard work but worth it moneywise!

while the passengers are tired and asleep

he starts singing the song, 'The Tibetan Plateau'

门

那白天黑夜都敞开的
大门，就是死亡

而双脚能够进进出出的
门，那是家门

人们踏上公共汽车的
门，但还能下来

而死亡是世间运行不息
并把每一个人当作停靠站的

那辆公共汽车的门
你只能上去一次

The Door

the gate, open day and
night, is death

and the door, where the feet can get in
and out, is the door of home

people embark on a bus
by its door but they can disembark

while death is the door
to the bus that never stops operating

and takes each person as a stop
where you can only embark once

深入

满城是雾，你怎么深入？
一个公司小职员
总算熬到了下午四点
班车上的瞌睡，把他
归还给空落了一天的小家

班车轮胎在雾中滑行
你感到有波浪袭来
你不想深入，也深入不了
外交部大楼像巨大的蜂巢
蜜蜂似的机密在那儿嗡嗡响

软体的雾，裹住城市的铁
有几棵银杏树已经枯死
剩下的也活得憔悴
参观十三陵墓穴的游客
没能察觉死亡：挨得太近

满城是雾。你怎么深入？
前后左右都是人。一些车

冲了过去，另一些小心翼翼
护城河铲除了淤泥，铺上了
水泥砖：那些泥鳅怎么深入？

Penetrating

when the city is full of fog, how can you penetrate into it?

when a petty company clerk

manages to get through the day till 4pm

the sleep on the bus returns him

to his petty home that remains empty all day

as the wheels of the bus are rolling through the fog

you feel the coming of the waves

you don't want to, nor can you, penetrate into them

the building of Foreign Ministry resembles a huge hive

where secrets, like bees, are buzzing

the soft fog is wrapping up the iron of the city

where a number of ginkgo trees have died of withering

the remaining ones alive but haggard

tourists who visit the Ming Tombs

are not aware of death as they are so close to it

and the city is full of fog. How can you ever penetrate into it?

surrounded by people on all sides. A number of vehicles

have rushed through it and a number of others are doing so with caution

the city moat, its silt dredged up, has been laid

with cement bricks: how can those loaches penetrate it?

习静

为苇岸而作

1. 街上

四月。我来到街上,
离开了公园。
公园安静,
因为我的心安静。
但十点钟以后,公园里
安静是一个谜。

这安静里究竟有什么?
街上只剩下人影、纸片、痰迹……

嗞嗞响的灯雾。
我在大街上瞎转。
事情,在口舌间
变得更加暧昧。

2. 桃花

四月是一个兆头。
艳肥的桃花只为自己发情。

逛动物园的，有孩子也有大人，
还有一只波斯猫
从妇人怀里
窜进草丛。

四月是一个线头，
穿过事情的针眼。

四月。动物、植物发情。
幸福的桃花在必败的途中，
忙着把自己的蕊打开。

3. 我

我迟迟疑疑，不敢
靠近桃花，更不敢
伸手去摘！

但众多桃花骤然
开屏，我结巴，我
迟疑，我我我……

我跟随一只蜻蜓，
在河沿，一圈儿
一圈儿地飞。

4. 四月

四月那么小，
像一朵桃花那么小，
四月用它低弱的呼吸
喊：嫩芽，嫩芽，嫩芽！
但四月太小了！
像一缕风，一闪，
就飞远了。
四月那么弱，
像嫩芽那么弱，
像襁褓里的婴儿那么弱，
但从嫩芽里源源不断地
分泌出小小的
青涩的愿望……

这愿望太苦了！

它秘密，胆怯。
不能告诉任何人！

5. 针

一根针刺疼了心，
又跑掉了！
像摔到地上的泪，
再也找不着影儿。

心啊它只能藏到花蕊里，
只能在蜜蜂到来之前
转移到针尖上。
心啊它颤抖着，到处寻找
它没有屋顶的居住地。

它尽情地，不为人知地，
哭！因为太纯洁，
太善。

6. 泪

一小滴泪爬出了幽深的眼窝，
在脸颊上做一次湿漉漉的长途旅行。

它摔碎了，因为太沉。
它挂不住，因为脸上没有吊钩。

一滴泪太抒情了！
后面跟着花瓣的大部队。

再也不可能返回。

7. 疾病

四月。我每天若有所思。
墙上挂着爱情，体内生长着病。
句子跟着我，到处找药。

脸，屡次被词语划破！
进城，出城，躲躲闪闪。
但还是被记忆——这个贼，
翻了出来。

一天像一把锁。
锁里活着真实。

忘光了，但又谈论。
糊涂着，因为还爱。

我总是那么含蓄，那么痛心！
唉，再说吧。

其实我再也不会去说它。
一条命从天秤上折断了，
因为另一头太沉。

事情发生了！
我只好：习静。
四月，我每天真有所失。

8. 死

接到死亡通知单的朋友，
先是慌了神，然后挺直腰杆，
扳着指头掐算
命运已掐算过的余生。

远远地，我挂念着，眼看着
他的形体他的骨和他的血肉
一天天塌陷。

明天太阳还会升起。
明天还能见到你吗？
肉身是一次性的。

这个人还爱着。
这个人的心还在急跳。
这个人死后将被邻居反复提起。

但很快，心跳就弱了，
弱下去了……
在五月的一天。

掀开内衣，时间
并无身体。除了疼痛
他，比活着时还活着。

9. 默想

我以前常默想垂危者的心境，

后来我东南西北地跑，到处是风景。
我翻开一本书，就再也合不拢，
我的内心迷茫，先是海，后是浪花……

我手中拎着草药，忘了目的地。
碎土覆盖骨灰，我拎着一双空手归来。

四月清楚四月是要过去的。
麦田躺着，哭泣着：松驰，柔软。

我和我们，又回到日常生活的喧闹中，
喧闹——这日常生活的肥皂泡！

Getting Used to Quietness

for Wei An

1. On the Street

April. I've arrived in a street,

having left a park.

the park is quiet,

because my heart is quiet.

but, after 10am, the quietness of the park

is a riddle.

what is there in the quietness?

there are only human shadows, pieces of paper, traces of spittle on the

    street...

the hissing lamp fog.

I turn around blindly on the street.

things become even more ambiguous

between my tongue and my mouth.

2. The Peach Flowers

April is a sign.
the fat flowers are having estrus only for themselves.

kids and adults are strolling in the park,
as well as a Persian cat
who jumps into the grass
from the arms of a woman.

April is a thread
that goes through the needle-eye of things.

April. Animals. Plants with estrus.
the happy peach flowers, on the way to defeat,
are busy opening their own stamen.

3. I

I hesitate, but I dare not
approach the flowers, and even less do I dare
pick them!

but the mass of them, all of a sudden
display their feathers, I stammer and I
hesitate, I–I–I–...

I follow a dragonfly

that flies along the river

turning in circles

4. April

April is so small

as small as a peach flower

April cries out

with its weak breathings: Tender bud, tender bud, tender bud!

but April is so small!

like a breeze that, in a flash

is gone

April is so weak

as weak as a tender bud

as weak as a baby swaddled up

but that manages to emit

a green and astringent wish

continuously from the buds...

such a bitter wish!

it's so secretive and timid

it can't be revealed to anyone!

5. The Needle

a needle pains the heart
and is gone!
like a drop of tear that dashes itself on the ground
its shadow unfindable

oh, heart that can only hide itself in the heart of a flower
will transfer itself to the tip of the needle
before the arrival of the bees

oh, heart that shivers everywhere in search
of the resident without a roof

it cries, to its heart's content
unbeknownst to anyone as it's so pure
so good.

6. Tears

a tiny teardrop creeps out of the deep eye socket
making a wet journey across the cheek

when it, too heavy, breaks itself
there is no hook on the face to hang it with

such a lyrical teardrop!

followed by the troop of flowers

no longer able to return

7. The illness

April. Daily, I seem deep in thought

love hanging on the wall as illness is growing inside me

lines follow me, looking for medications everywhere

my face, scarred by the words on numerous occasions!

going into, and out of, the city, dodging

but still getting dug out

by the memory: a thief

the day is like a lock

in which truth lives

forgetting everything but still talking

confused, because still in love

I always am so subtle, so grieved

well, let's talk about it some other time

I won't, though, talk about it again
a life breaks up on the balance scale
because the other end is too heavy

something happens!
I have to get used to the quietness
in April, I really am lost, daily

8. Death

friends who received the death notice
panicked and straightened themselves
counting on their fingers
the rest of the years that Fate has counted

in a distance, I keep missing him, watching
his figure, his bones, and his flesh and blood
collapsing day by day

the sun will rise again tomorrow
but will I see you again?
the body is only a one-off

this person is still in love
this person's heart still beats

this person, after he dies, will be mentioned, again and again, by his
neighbours

but, soon, his heartbeats weaken
weakening...
on a day in May

when you lift his underclothes, time
has no body except the pain
and he, more alive than when he's alive

9. Contemplation

I used to contemplate the mental state of a dying person
then I ran north, south, west and east, and there's landscape everywhere

when I open a book, it won't close again
my heart at sea; first it's the ocean, then the waves...

herbal medications in hand, I forgot the destination
broken earth over the bone ashes, I returned, empty-handed

April knows that April will leave
the wheatfield lies prostrate, crying: relaxed, and soft

I and us, going back to the commotion of ordinary life

the commotion: the soap bubbles of an ordinary life!

颤抖

它颤抖
我跟着颤抖
大楼，我

大地颤抖
洗衣机甩干时颤抖
刚掏出的鱼内脏颤抖
被面包车撞得飞出去的
农村妇女的嘴角颤抖
我跟着颤抖
大地，我

天空颤抖
它的丝绸被闪电撕破
孩子颤抖
他发高烧已经三天
小偷颤抖
他的脖子凉嗖嗖
立交桥颤抖
载重卡车正隆隆驶过

废墟颤抖
时间唱着凯旋歌
心脏颤抖
死亡掐紧了喉管
我跟着颤抖
天空，我

亲人
在病床上颤抖
我跟着颤抖
我，我，我……

Trembling

it trembles

as I tremble

the building, I

the land trembles

the washing machine trembles when tumbling dry

the insides of a fish, just disemboweled, tremble

the corner of the mouth of a countrywoman trembles

as she flies off on collision with the minibus

I tremble with it

the land, I

the sky trembles

its silk rent by the lightning

the child trembles

having been in a high fever for 3 days

the thief trembles

his neck feeling the cold

the overpass trembles

as a truck, heavily loaded, is rumbling across it

the ruins tremble

as time is singing a triumphant song

the heart trembles

when death is tightening its grip on the throat
along with it I tremble
the sky, I

my loved one
trembles in the sick bed
and I tremble, too
I, I, I...

秋日杂记

1

风像软刀子
在衣袖上飘
阳光喝醉了
躺在空地上

秋天冒烟的味儿
烤羊肉串那么香
一直飘到了新疆……

树叶一片接一片
落下来。有位老人
枯坐一旁，双手
摩挲着瘦膝上的残年

但树叶，还是
一片接一片，落下来
好像自己愿意

2

大地上秋日朗朗
对这生命的轮回
一棵树只能接受

落叶的心情也不相同
有几张晒太阳
有几张追行人
还有几张，迷了路
一头撞到电线杆上

风把它们翻过去又翻过来
像不识字的儿童硬要看书

我走路时像
被什么绊了一下
我停下来，等一个朋友
突然，白杨树飒飒乱响
接着便有人拍我的肩膀

3

秋日，你要静心
走自己的路

你要一心一意
想到什么就忘掉什么
你还要去看，去听
做这些都要用心

看着干干净净的阳光
我也想活得干干净净
听着天地间隐约的风声
我的脸就成了眼泪的晒谷场

又一阵风吹来
这么多飞翔的精灵
沦落尘世！你一边
发呆，一边心生悲悯

这么美的日子，你
却受不了

4
幽深的庭院凭幽深
守住那棵柿子树
柿子都跑市场上去了
枝干和枯叶留了下来

光阴走得寂寞
孩子们活蹦乱跳

慈爱的老人凭慈爱
照看满地的儿童
中年人各忙各的
几乎忘记了童年

是秋风使他们
偶尔回过头来

5

一阵寒颤：你顿时感到
每个汗毛孔都满了秋凉
凉，比老中医摸得更准

暮色提前来敲门
像三十五岁的你
迎接挡不住的白头发

我郁闷地走在幸福大街上
好多面孔仿佛昨日见过
一切漠然：无激动，无争吵

娘喊儿子的尖嗓音
把暮色拖长了——
水圈儿似地，扩散开去

6
除了一阵寒颤
双手像两只眼睛
一样没有把握

这个秋天染上了
不要命的灵魂色
你动用右手，捂住胸口

心啊，你在尘世间
究竟想要什么？你
比你想象的要更真实
没有一个细节漏过你

7
十字路口，昏沉
扭秧歌锣鼓，热腾腾
飘带红绸翻起了尘土
老槐树一再被冷落

推土机逼近了
一堵破墙没推就倒

墙角，落叶越聚越多
比一床大棉被还要厚
一窝小老鼠得了温暖

走一段弯路，你
找到了家。舍掉几个
字，意思更完整了

我来到世上是因祸得福

8
屋子里，声音越来越杂
干什么或不干什么
现在都由不得你
落叶催促枝上的残叶
一棵树迟早得光秃秃

据说有一些树四季常青
它们的秋天更不易察觉
越来越僻静的屋子

你内心深处的安宁

幽深而悲苦
闲静而乐观

9
十年前，你顺着山沟
上香山。生活的折扇
也是在那一年打开

如今多少风已从扇面上掠过
多少枫叶从树根又回到枝头

太极拳，太极拳
师傅已经仙逝——
胃癌蚕食了每一寸
肉的土地，因为疼
他最后信了不死的神

此刻的秋天浑身无一朵云彩

Miscellaneous Notes on an Autumn Day

1

the wind, like a soft knife

is blowing on the sleeves

the sun, drunken

lies on an empty lot

the smell of the autumn smoking

as fragrant as the lamb skewer

drifts till it reaches Xinjiang...

leaf after leaf

falls. An old man

sits idle, his hands

massaging the remaining years on his thin knees

but the leaves still fall

one by one

as if willing themselves

2

the autumn is bright and light on the land

all a tree can ever do

is accept this transmigration of life

the mood of the fallen leaves is also different
some sunning themselves
some chasing after the pedestrians
and a few others, having lost their way
hit headlong against the telephone pole

the wind is turning them over and over again
like kids who insist on reading a book whose words they don't know

while I, walking
stumbled over something
so I stopped, to wait for a friend
on a sudden, the white poplars started making a soughing noise
when someone patted on my shoulder

3
on this autumn day, you have to calm down
taking to your own path
you have to be single-minded
forgetting anything that you happen to think of
and you have to look and listen
doing all that with attention

looking at the clean sunlight
I, also, would like to live in a clean manner

and listening to the faint sound of the wind between heaven and earth
my face turns into a grain-sunning ground for tears

another wind comes blowing
so many flying angels
that have fallen onto this earth! You remain
dazed, as sympathy is growing in your heart

such a beautiful day, too much
for you to stand

4

the deeply quiet courtyard, with its deep quietness
keeps the persimmon tree
whose persimmons have all gone to the market
leaving the trunk and the withered leaves behind

time is walking at a solitary pace
while kids are alive and kicking

kind old men, by way of kindness
look after the kids all over the place
while the middle-aged men are busy with their separate affairs
seemingly oblivious to their own childhood
it is the autumn wind that occasionally
turns their heads around

5

a shivering and you feel

that every pore is filled with the autumn chill

the chill, more accurate than an old traditional Chinese doctor

dusk knocks on your door, ahead of time

like you, at 35

who has to welcome the greying hair, unstoppable

feeling depressed, I walk on the happy street

many of the faces I seem to have seen yesterday

are indifferent: neither excited nor querulous

the shrill voice in which Mother calls her son

elongates the evening—

expanding, like the circles in the water

6

apart from the shivering

the hands are as unsure

as the eyes

the autumn is dyed with

the reckless colour of the soul

you cover your chest, with your right hand

ah, heart, what do you really want
in this world? You

are more real than what you imagine
no detail escaping you

7
at the crossroads, a dizzy
yangko dance, and a red silk ribbon
is raising the dust

the pagoda tree is once again given the cold shoulder
the bulldozer is getting close
a broken wall falls by itself without being pushed

in one corner, the fallen leaves pile up
thicker than a big quilt
where a brood of mice secure warmth

having taken a detour, you
find your home. When a few words
are removed, the meaning is more complete
my very coming to this world is a blessing in disguise

8

in the room, the voices become more and more mixed

you don't have any choice

to do or not to do

the fallen leaves are urging the remaining ones to leave

a tree, sooner or later, will have to be stripped bare

they say there are evergreens

whose autumn is less detectable

the increasingly quiet room

the quietness in your heart of hearts

deeply quiet and bitterly sad

leisurely tranquility and optimism

9

10 years ago you walked up the Fragrant Hill

along the valley and it was in that year that the folded fan of life

unfolded itself

so much wind has since blown across the fan

so many maple leaves have again returned to their branches from their

    roots

Tai Chi Boxing, Tai Chi Boxing

the Master has died—

the stomach cancer has eroded every inch

of the land of flesh and, because of the pain

he ended up believing in the undying deity

the autumn, at this very moment, has not a single cloud about it

旅行

太阳，给刚刚睡醒的山脊线
也刷刷牙吧

长途车破得像一堆烂铁
哒哒哒……发动机终于摇响了

司机精瘦：一只瘦猴
售票员是一个大大咧咧的北京丫头

司机，售票员，乘客：共4人
我们哐当哐当上路了

"路上可得好好拣些人……"

油门踩到底，轮胎直哼哼
整个车身疯抖，像立马要散架

早起的农民，赶着骡子
车架垒满砖头，慢成蜗牛

过节的人们拎着大包小包
路旁有那么多人等着进城

那北京丫头高兴得直发愁——
只见她同司机嘀咕了几声

汽车便冲进人堆，嘎的一声
急停。糟糕！车门打不开了

"推一下，使劲儿推……"
"哎呀，我的鞋掉了……"

"中国人过节就是挤！"

有位大姑娘羞得涨红了脸
有个小伙子猛推她的后腰

折腾烦了，司机想走
那北京丫头突然喊开了——

"等一等，还有我妈呢！
我妈说好了在这儿等的……"

这乖闺女还在往窗外喊呢
一个粗嗓门从车罐头里炸响了

"小月，小月，妈在这儿哪！"

敢情！这粗壮有力的老妈
早已独自攻上这小山头了

挤得要死，却喜气洋洋
汽车猛一拐，冲上高速路

西三旗，清河镇，马甸桥……
太阳晒烫我的半边脸和一只耳朵

秋收黄灿灿。玉米们
拥挤着，趴在农家屋顶上

我瞥了一眼坐在身旁的妻子
她脑袋歪在我肩上瞌睡得正香

长途车摇摇晃晃，晃晃摇摇
屁股后头，喷吐一路黑烟……

The Journey

will you, the sun, brush the teeth
for the mountain ridge that has just woken up?

the long-distance coach was so rundown it's like a heap of scrap iron
the engine, rattling for a long time, before it started running

the monkey of a driver: razor-thin
and the conductor, a slaphappy Beijing girl

4 in all: the driver, the conductor and the passengers
as we went clanging out on the road

'we'll have to pick handfuls of people on the way...'

as the driver stepped all the way down on the accelerator, the tyres grunted
and the vehicle vibrated, ready to fall apart any moment

an early-riser peasant was driving a mule
his cart heaped with bricks, at a snail's pace

people, to celebrate the festivity, were carrying their bags, big and small
so many of them waiting on the roadside to get into the city

the Beijing girl was so happy that she got worried—
she whispered something into the driver's ear

as the bus rushed into the crowd, coming to a screeching
stop. Shit! The door refused to open

'push, give it a hard push...'
'oh, no, my shoes have come off my feet...'

'a Chinese festive occasion is always too crowded!'

a girl was so shy her face turned red
as a young man gave her a rough shove at the back

much bored with people-handling, the driver was about to get on the way
when the Beijing girl started yelling—

'wait! Mom is coming
as she said she'd be here...'

the good girl was still yelling
when a loud voice exploded in the can of a bus

'Xiao Yue, Xiao Yue, Mom is here!'

why, of course! The old mum, stout and strong
had taken the hill all by herself

happy, though almost squeezed to death
in a sharp turn, the bus rushed onto the freeway

West Three Flag, Clean River Town, Horse Pasture Bridge...
the sun hot on my cheek and ear

the autumn harvest golden. Bunches of corn
lay, prone and crowded, on the roof of the peasants' houses

I glanced at my wife, sitting next to me
soundly asleep, and her head on my shoulder

the long-distance coach shook and lurched
its arse leaving a black plume of smoke behind...

梦中

终于，我没有被掏空。
终于，我摔了一跤。

……喘不过气来！我的
全部力量只为了一声喊。

呼喊声已冲到了喉咙口，
但被大张着的嘴给堵住了。

又是恶梦！疯跑的游戏。
我像个贼，在长廊上，追……

好像有人出门，什么也没说。
我一下子明白了：那种眼神。

我去追……像去救一条命！
全部力量只为了一声喊。

喊出一声就行了，那个人
回一下头就没事了……

醒了！醒了就不好玩了。
我一边早餐，一边回味。

梦中我究竟想对谁喊？
为什么声音没喊出就哑了？

为什么一眨眼就过了火海？
我能对此作何解释！

也许天花板目睹了一切，
但天花板是一张闭紧的嘴。

怎样才能醒来却还梦着？
那是被恐惧掐紧的喉咙。

In the Dream

I didn't end up being gutted
but I did end up in a fall

...breathless! All my strength
lay in a yell

as sound rose to my throat
when it was stopped by my gaping mouth

another nightmare! A game of running wildly
in which I was a thief, chasing along the corridor...

someone, it seems, was going out, saying nothing at all
I understood the way he looked

I gave chase...as if to rescue someone's life
all my strength for the purpose of a yell

it would do when it came forth and if the guy
turned his head back things would be fine...

I woke up! It's no fun when one wakes up
I was having my breakfast while tasting the aftertaste of the dream

who did I intend to shout at in the dream?
why did I go mute even before the sound came forth?

how did I cross the sea of fire in the twinkling of an eye?
how do I explain all that?

the ceiling may have witnessed all that
but it's a mouth, tightly shut

how can one have been in the dream while he's awake?
but that's the throat closely held by fears

有一只蟑螂正在死去

"有一只蟑螂正在死去！"
妻子大声喊。

我跑过去一看，确实有
一只大蟑螂，仰面躺着，

它使出吃奶的劲，
想把身子翻过来。

看来它中了毒。

"可怜的蟑螂正在死去……"
妻子不安地咕哝。

我白了她一眼——昨天是
她非要我去买"死得快"。

这只大蟑螂正在死去，
而且它很快就会死去。

这正是我们想要的结局。

我蹲下身，仔细观察。
妻子站着，露一脸恻隐。

看来它已经没救了。

我们出了厨房，
各忙各的事儿。

There's a Dying Cockroach

'there's a dying cockroach!'
my wife shouted out loud

I ran over and saw there really was
a huge cockroach, lying on its back

making every effort
to turn itself over

it seemed that it was poisoned

'the poor cockroach is dying...'
my wife muttered, with discomfort

I gave her a dirty look—it was yesterday
that she insisted I go and buy 'Die Quick'

the huge cockroach was dying
and would die shortly

an end that we were both hoping for

I squatted and looked at it closely
while my wife stood, her face filled with pity

it's obvious that it's hopeless

we went out of the kitchen
each occupied with our own affairs

整个下午"啪"一声碎了

整个下午"啪"一声碎了——
好像隐身人在喊：人类啊，醒醒！

恐惧的气味，从鼻孔一直潜入内心，
周围都是雾，人群被人群裹着。

晚上九点。街上只剩下几丛树影，
一股尘土从街口腾起，又颓然坐下。

这个四月到底怎么了——
桃花开到一半就谢了？

这个世纪到底怎么了——
好好的肺突然就干咳起来？

传染病！是肺结核复活了
它那张后现代的脸："非典"——

但没有人能读懂！它本身像处方，
只是，开处方的老中医去哪儿找？

每一个家庭有每一个家庭的担心。
生活这个词像一只船开始漏水。

我们都在船上：我们，每一个！
救人！自救！必须把勇气挖出来。

谁能真正帮我们度过这个难关？
人啊又到了该反省的时候了——

为什么生活会弄得那么复杂？
瞎子们高举着灯泡有什么用？

命运之书正被虚无之手缓缓打开，
抱着这个下午，人啊你无处可躲。

整个下午"啪"一声碎了——
惊而坐起，仿佛一条命倒塌。

窗外，天空如常，并无碎片。
也许，处变不惊的只有时间。

The Whole Afternoon Broke Apart with a Crack

the whole afternoon broke apart with a crack—
as if an invisible man was shouting: Wake up, Mankind!

the smell of fear crept from the nose into my heart of hearts
fog everywhere, people wrapping people up

9pm. The street was left with clusters of tree shadows
a trail of dust rose from the intersection before it slumped into a sitting
     position

what on earth happened to this April—
the peach flowers fell even before they were half open

what on earth happened to this century—
why did the good lungs burst into dry coughing?

an infectious disease! It's the revival of tuberculosis
with its postmodern face: SARS—

that no one could understand, like a prescription
one that the old Chinese herbal doctor would search for in vain

each family has its own concerns

life, the word, resembles a ship that begins leaking

we are all on board: every one of us!

save all! Save ourselves! One must dig out courage

who can help us pull through?

man, it's time you questioned yourself again

why has life gotten so complicated?

and what's the point with the blind people raising high their light bulbs?

the book of fate is being slowly opened by the hand of nihility

embracing this afternoon when no one can escape anywhere

the whole afternoon broke apart with a crack—

one sits up with a start as if a life had collapsed

outside the window, the sky remains the same, no fragments

perhaps time is the only thing that keeps calm

咳嗽

还没到十点。离
晚间新闻还有一段
不算太短的等待

咳嗽冲上来了！像
涨潮一样无法控制，像
叫醒服务一样准时

喉咙胀得痒痒。痒
痒得发疯！但痒的
感觉，怎么也咳不出来

活在红尘里，谁
不想一醉？酒，酒……
干杯，干杯！

趁着醉的暗门半开
你我，把各自的内心
掏出来，亮了一下

咳嗽是心事的反复
播放。太阳，你
照见的秘密太多了

生活的力量，就是
让人心碎。散步，散步
……然后，分手

当一位农村少女低声
说出：堕落！当咳嗽
活像一位浪漫主义大师

你我，只能把理想
降到弯腰的高度，并把
肾虚症，当众揭发出来

Coughing

not yet 10. Still quite a long way
from
the evening news

coughing comes on, like
the rising tide that's uncontrollable, like
the morning call that is on time

the throat is itchy, so itchy
it drives one crazy, but the itchy
sensation one can't cough out

living in the red dust, who
doesn't want to get drunk? Liquor, liquor...
bottoms up, bottoms up!

while the dark door of drunkenness remains ajar
you and I, let's reveal our heart of hearts
by digging it out

coughing is but a repetitive broadcasting
of heart matters. The sun, you
have shone on so many secrets

the power of life is meant
to break hearts. Walking and walking
...till one breaks up

when a country girl says
in a low voice: Fallen! When coughing
is like a romantic master

all you and I can do is bend the ideal
to the height of a bent back while exposing
the kidney deficiency to the public

门

打了好几次，最后
打开了，门里
是一片乱码

门里没有人，只有
乱码，这是我
没有想到的

铁打的门，我用
手打，嘭嘭嘭
没人回答

嘭嘭，门是虚掩的
像一句广告词
像包装纸

广告是一扇暗门
广告词的写作
模仿做诗

写作总没有活着
更难变化
更难

变化，变化，门
两扇变成一扇
招小偷

一扇，又一扇
关拢，或打开
都是门

The Door

trying to open it a few times till
it was finally opened but behind the door
there was a spread of garbled message texts

no one there, just
garbled message texts, more than I
had expected

an iron-door that I knocked
with my hand, banging, banging, banging
no answer

banging and banging, but the door was ajar
like an advertising phrase
like packing paper

advertising is a hidden door
and the advertising phrase
imitates the writing of poetry

writing, compared with living
finds it harder to change
and is harder

change, change, the door

with two halves that turn into one

inviting thieves

one half, another half

they close or open

both are part of the door

门

从它那儿进
从它那儿出
一进一出
门吱嗯

门里面有门
门外面有门
门里门外
全是门

关着门数钱
开着门干活
门门门门
木头门

铜锁挂在门上
钥匙响在腰间
没锁没钥匙
是棺材

天是最大的门
打开后是空的
猜一猜谁是
守门人

The Door

entering by it

exiting by it

entrance and exit

cause the door to groan

a door inside the door

a door outside the door

inside and outside the door

there are all doors

counting money with the door closed

doing work with the door open

door, door, door and door

wooden doors

the copper lock hanging on the door

the keys noisy on the waist

neither the lock nor the keys

mean the coffin

the sky is the biggest door

when opened, it's empty

guess who is

the doorkeeper

门

我想再做一扇门
我知道你买了房子

刚刚找到刨子
这扇门已经做好了

还没伸手去推
它就吱嗯应了一声

这扇门有小小的魔力
你会喜欢走进走出

这扇门不是木头做的
跟钢铁也没有关系

你需要这么一扇门
因为你买了房子

就把这扇门送给你吧
这样你会感到安全

这样你可以开始搬家
对，把整个家都搬进去

家：一个多么怪的人
进了门他才肯坐下

找到一扇门几乎
就找到了一个家

这扇门就叫家门吧
别忘了给它装一把锁

The Door

I'd like to make another door
as I know that you've bought a house

I've just found a plane
the door is now made

even before I push it
it groans in reply

the door has such a tiny magic power
that you like to walk in and out of it

the door is not made from wood
nor has it got anything to do with steel

you need such a door
because you've bought a house

then let me give a door away to you
so you can feel safe

and can begin moving house
right, to move all your family-home in

home: what a strange person he is
for he will only sit down when he enters into the door

once you find a door you have almost
found a home

let's call it the door of home
and remember to fix a lock on it

竹晶之疼

疼过之后，那滩血就空了。
水泥地，冷冰冰地吸纳了它。

如今，只剩下那疼过的疼，
还在那空里，延伸着它的空。

无数双脚在街上走动，
手里拎着蔬菜，或排骨。

那肉身真的升向天庭了吗？
我不信。但竹晶，她信！

那灵魂真的跳出躯壳了吗？
竹晶信。但我，不信！

竹晶是飞走的！但只
飞了一小会儿就触地了。

太疼！躺在地上动不了！
除了死神，谁也动不了她。

轻轻一动，就会要她的命。
急救车来了：竹晶走了。

她在用最后的呼吸，说
疼疼疼疼疼疼疼疼疼……

非人的疼！要命的疼！
活着的人无从想象的疼！

血肉疼糊涂了，骨头疼
麻痹了，嘴还在试着说出

疼：竹晶把疼留了下来。
这是她事先没料到的。

不！她事先什么都想过了。
她甚至也把死留了下来。

她知道有人会谈起她，
她用死同我们活在一起。

她是圆的，她是空的。
圆摔碎了，空又满了。

谁，含着泪，通过竹晶，
又一次讲述了生死无常？

有几双耳朵听见？生命中
真正的疼，只有一次。

那疼，如今藏在水泥地下，
那死，如今存在骨灰盒里。

The Pain of Zhujing

after the pain, the pool of blood was empty
the cement floor, icily, taking it all in

now, the pain that was pained remains
in the emptiness, extending the emptiness

countless feet are moving on the street
hands carrying vegetables or pork ribs

has the body really ascended to heaven?
Zhujing thinks so although I don't

has the soul really jumped out of its shell?
Zhujing thinks so although I don't

Bamboo Crystal (Zhujing) had flown away! But only
for a brief moment before she touched the ground

so painful! Not stirring, lying on the ground
no one could move her except Death

one slight movement would kill her
the ambulance came: Zhujing was gone

breathing her last, she said

pain pain pain pain pain pain pain pain pain...

unearthly pain! Killing pain!

the pain no living could imagine!

flesh and blood were so painful they were confused, and the bones pained

numbed, the mouth was trying to say

pain: Zhujing left the pain behind

something she had not expected

but no! She had thought of everything

she had even kept death behind

she knew people would talk about her

she lived with us through death

she is round and she is empty

the roundness has dashed into pieces and the emptiness is filled

who is it, tearful, that once again tells of life and death

through Zhujing?

how many ears have heard it? In life

real pain comes but only once

the pain, now hidden below the cement floor

the death, now kept in the box of ashes

如果可以

如果可以，
我想戒了爱。

如果可以，
我想不出生。

如果可以，
我想不长大。

如果可以，
我想从头再活一次。

如果可以，
我想亲手宰了你。

如果可以，
我想搬到月亮上去住。

如果可以，
我想把心摘给你。

如果可以，
我想做一粒小米虫。

如果可以，
我想让钟表歇一歇。

如果可以，
我想跟上帝谈一谈。

如果可以，
我想到天堂瞧一眼。

如果可以，
我想去地狱转一圈。

如果可以，
我想成为我。

但我又想，这些
都是不可以的。

如果可以，
我想让这些都可以。

但这些都是不可以的。

但我说的是如果可以。

If I Could

if I could
I would quit love

if I could
I would rather not be born

if I could
I would refuse to grow up

if I could
I would like to relive my life from the very beginning

if I could
I would like to kill you with my own hands

if I could
I'd like to move to the moon

if I could
I'd like to pluck my heart for you

if I could

I'd like to turn into a tiny rice bug

if I could

I'd like to give the clocks and watches a break

if I could

I'd like to talk with God

if I could

I'd like to go to heaven for a look

if I could

I'd like to go to hell for a visit

if I could

I'd like to become myself

but then again I don't think
these things are possible

if I could

I'd like to make them all possible

but none of these are possible

but I've said *If I could*

吼哈

两个老头
在公园晨练
一个老头
前后转腰
一个老头
大声吼哈
两个老头
相距三米
你看着我
我看着你

一个老头
继续吼哈
一吼一哈
声若滚雷
一个老头
听得心烦
说你别再
吼哈个没完

一个老头
停了吼哈
起了怒火
这是公园
你管得着吗
你吃饱了
撑的说完
把头一甩
接着吼哈

一个老头
听了之后
实在生气
一边转腰
一边回击
你影响我
我就要管
我管的就是
你这样的人

两个老头
就这么嚷嚷
就这么斗嘴

一个六十
一个七十
一个胖点
一个瘦点
都是爷爷
都是前辈
不想动手
只能动嘴

旁边有人
走过跑过
并不停下
做个调解
就我一个
在不远处
坐石头上
听他们斗嘴
看他们脸色

见没人理
一个老头
吼哈一声
扬长而去

一个老头
转了转腰
哼了一哼
掉头也走
只剩下我
原地目送

Roaring with a 'Ho' and a 'Ha'

two old men

are having morning exercises in the park

one is twisting at the waist

the other is roaring, uttering the sound of a 'ho' and a 'ha'

the two old men

keeping a distance of three metres between them

look at

each other

an old man

keeps 'ho'ing and 'ha'ing

like

a rolling thunder

the other old man

annoyed

says: Can you stop

'ho'ing and 'ha'ing please?

the old man

having stopped 'ho'ing and 'ha'ing

is furious

with a grunt

leaving me alone

watching them go

谁是谁

谁是谁？
我怎么知道！

你是谁？
你问我我问谁！

生死一杯酒。
这杯酒谁酿的？

谁是你谁是我，
你我成了夫妻。

谁醒着谁睡了，
都是一呼一吸。

你究竟是谁？
你爱谁谁！

你爱谁？爱谁之后
你还爱过谁？

"爱自由！"风
一闪，就飞远了。

谁会谁也不爱？
你总是谁的谁。

那个谁是谁？
你愿意你是谁？

"自己！"自己又是
谁？谁是谁的谁？

即便你哭喊，
还是不能惊动谁。

即便你跳楼，
还是不能成全谁。

谁刚刚出生？
谁已经死了？

生前是谁？死后是谁？
生死之间又是谁？

腐烂的，是谁？
复活的，又是谁？

也许无人复活！
只有谁让谁复活。

谁活着谁就有戏。
谁又在重演谁的戏？

谁是谁的谁？
你爱谁谁！

莫非有诗——
谁是谁，等

找到另一棵树
才能验证。

Who's Who?

who's who?
how do I know?

who are you?
who else can I ask if you ask me?

life and death are but a cup of wine
but who's the one who has brewed it?

who are you and who am I?
you and I have become husband and wife

who's asleep and who's awake?
both are breathing in and out

who on earth are you?
whoever you think it is it will be

who do you love? Who else have you loved
after whoever you loved?

'I love freedom!' The wind
with a flash, has flown
far away

whoever it is that will not love whoever else?
you always will be whose who

who's that who?
who would you like to be?

'self!' But who is
self? Who is whose who?

even if you cry
who can you stir?

even if you jump off a building
whose aim can you achieve?

who's just born?
who has already died?

who's it before birth? Who's it after death?
and who's it between life and death?

who's rotten?

who's resurrected?

perhaps no one is resurrected!

only who can resurrect whom

whoever alive is hopeful

who's replaying whose play?

who's whose who?

whoever you think it is it will be

or perhaps there is poetry—

who is who? If you want to find out, wait

till you find another tree

for proof

心里有烟

心里有烟，那很危险—
如果烟越来越大怎么办？
如果七窍被呛住了怎么办？

烟里有火，恐怕是暗火—
暗火灼心啊！千万别乱拨，
弄不好火会从汗毛孔蹿出来！

火里有劈啪声，有火星，
盯着一朵火焰一句话不说的人
肯定喝高了：他在流泪……

劈啪声里有鬼，女烟鬼！
女孩子抽大烟抽成个鬼似的—
她羞红的脸已被熏黄。

鬼里有情，人鬼情未了！
多少人爱着爱着就成了鬼—
成了鬼，他们还要爱。

情里有爱，像木头里
有火。火旺了烟就没了，
火熄了木炭还在一阵阵冒烟。

爱里又有什么呢？有心—
空心人无心人怎么会有爱呢？
但心字里面是空的无的。

心里有烟，也不用怕—
打开心门，把烟放出来！
张开嘴巴，把话说出来！

There's Smoke in the Heart

it's dangerous if there's smoke in the heart—
what if the smoke gets worse?
what if the Seven Apertures are choked?

there is fire in the smoke, possibly a hidden fire—
oh, the hidden fire scorches the heart! Never poke it
or else the fire may leap out of the pores!

there's a crackling noise in the fire and there are sparkles
the guy who stares at a flame without saying a word
must have drunk himself high: he's in tears...

there's a devil in the crackling noise, a female devil of a smoker!
the girl has smoked herself into a devil—her flushed face smoked yellow

there's love in the devil, endless love between a being and a devil
so many have loved till they turn into devils—
even then they still love

there's emotion in love, like fire
in the wood. When the fire roars, the smoke is gone
when the fire is out, the embers are still smoking

what is there in love? There's heart—

how can a man with a hollow heart or a non heart love?

but inside the word 心 (heart), there is emptiness and nothing

there's smoke in the heart. Have no fear—

open its door, to let out the smoke!

open the mouth, to let out the words!

心里有烟

心里有烟，
心里有鬼，
心里有烟鬼。

男烟鬼？女烟鬼？

心里有火，
心里有灾，
心里有火灾。

救火车！救火车！

心里有怨，
心里有气，
心里有怨气。

开门，开窗，透气！

心里有情，
心里有人，
心里有情人。

成眷属？成冤家？

心里有数，
心里没数，
心里直打鼓。

一打鼓，烟跑了。

There's Smoke in the Heart

there's smoke in the heart

there are devils in the heart

there are smoking devils in the heart

male or female smoking devils?

there's smoke in the heart

there's a disaster in the heart

there's a fire disaster in the heart

fire truck! Fire truck!

there is rancour in the heart

there is anger in the heart

there's resentment in the heart

open the door! Open the window! Let in the air!

there's feeling in the heart

there's someone in the heart

there's someone loved in the heart

will that lead to family or enmity?

the heart knows

the heart doesn't

the heart thumps like a drum

and as soon as it does, the smoke escapes

这枯瘦肉身

我该拿这枯瘦肉身
怎么办呢？

答案或决定权
似乎都不在我手中。

手心空寂，如这秋风
一吹，掌纹能不颤动？

太阳出来一晒，
落叶们都服服帖帖。

牵挂这尘世，只欠
一位母亲的温暖——

比火焰低调，比爱绵长，
挽留着这枯瘦肉身。

任你逃到哪里，房屋
仍把你囚于四墙。

只好看天，漫不经心，
天色可由不得你。

走着出家的路，
走着回家的路……

我该拿什么来比喻
我与这枯瘦肉身的关系呢？

一滴水？不。一片叶？
不。一朵云？也不！

也许只是一堆干柴，
落日未必能点燃它，

但一个温暖的眼神，
没准就能让它烧起来，

烧成灰，烧成尘，
沿着树梢，飞天上去……

This Emaciated Body of Flesh

what am I going to do
with this emaciated body of flesh?

neither answer or decision
seems to be in my hand

my hand is quietly empty, like this autumn wind
that causes the palm prints to shiver when blowing across it

the sun, when out and shining
reduces the fallen leaves to submission

my concern with this dusty world lacks
the warmth of a mother—

lower-key than the fire and longer than love
that retains this emaciated body of flesh

wherever you escape, the house
imprisons you within the walls

the only option is to look up at the skies, carelessly
with no control over their colours

taking to the road out of home

taking to the road that leads to home

what analogy can I use

to describe my relationship to this emaciated body of flesh?

a drop of water? No. A leaf?

no. A cloud? Oh, no!

or perhaps a pile of dry wood

that the setting sun might not be able to set alight

but a warm look

is likely to set it afire

burning it to ashes, burning it to dust

causing it to fly skyward, along the crown of a tree...

北园

给明姬

北园。我小时候去过那里
　　那时北园尚未命名

它也许是我诞生的那座村庄
一声啼哭　撕破一片混沌
不　也许根本就没有哭声
凌晨三点　一切静悄悄的
一滴无辜生命　在草尖上　凝成

小时候　不推门就进了北园
我在一棵树下　做了两年梦
都是爬到天顶　然后啊一声
　　摔地上　惊醒

我的童年自由得像一只空碗
饥饿的眼前　米粒也发光

北园。自从诞生了明姬……
　　　从大自然，北园醒来

一颗忧心　催促她早熟
忧心如焚　燃烧成斑斓
她为什么要花十年笔墨呢—
收笔的刹那　她当然明白
北园没有门　北园不在北园

有人说　北园里什么都有
就是没有人　有人补充
树丛深处　有一些光
也有人说　她看见了死亡

北园。是梦？不是梦？
　　　请睁开眼，请闭上眼

────────

注：明姬，韩国大画家。《北园》是她的一幅5米×5米的巨画。

195

North Garden

for Myonghi

North Garden. I've been there when a child
    it's not named then

it may have been the village where I was born
a cry   that tore through the chaos
no there may never have been any cries
at 3am   all was quiet
a drop of an innocent life   formed on the tip of a grass

when I was little   I entered North Garden without pushing the door
under a tree   I dreamed for two years
in which I always climb to the top of the sky   before I uttered a cry
    and fell   waking myself up

my childhood was as free as an empty bowl
before the eyes of hunger   even grains of rice shined

North Garden. Since Kwai Fung Hin was born...
    North Garden woke up from Nature

196

a worrying heart urged her to grow ripe early

the heart burned, with anxiety, into splendors

why did she spend ten years of pen and ink—

the minute she put away her pen, she, of course, knew

that North Garden had no doors   and North Garden was not at North

Garden

some said   there was everything at North Garden

except people   some added

there was light   in the depths of the trees

and others said   she saw death

North Garden. Is it a dream? Is it no dream?

please open your eyes. Please close them.

Translator's note—*Myonghi, Korean artist.* North Garden *is a huge 5 by 5 metre painting of hers.*

因为/所以

因为有酒
所以喝
因为有醉
所以喝
因为地球旋转
所以摇滚
因为宇宙旋转
所以摇滚
月亮月亮
潮涨潮落
因为开心
所以大笑
哈哈哈哈
因为伤心
所以大哭
呜呜呜呜
长发长发
掀起波浪
因为喝高了
所以摇晃

因为西北风

所以发抖

因为摇啊摇

所以原地不动

因为梦

所以醒

因为道

所以德

因为针

所以扎

因为站着

所以没倒下

因为灯下

所以黑

因为阳光

所以晃眼

因为瞎了眼

所以心里明白

因为在

所以在

因为不在

所以在

因为脸色

所以铁青

因为电话

所以打

因为没人接

所以空打

因为只能这样

所以也就这样

因为没酒了

所以唱

轻轻哼吧

没有歌词

轻轻摇吧

大海困了

星星在

月亮也在

你不抬头

怎能看见

你不抬头

也能看见

你的心醉了

你的心起风了

风起于汗毛丛林处

风溺死在血脉大河

因为虚
所以无
因为虚无
所以万有
因为万有
所以虚无
因为不了
所以了之
你问因为
不答所以
因为因为
所以所以
哈哈哈哈
乐死我了
也乐死你

Because

because there's liquor
one drinks
because there's drunkenness
one drinks
because the earth rotates
one rocks and rolls
because the universe rotates
one rocks and rolls
the moon and the moon
the tide ebbs and flows
because delighted
one laughs
ha ha ha ha
because brokenhearted
one bursts into tears
oh oh oh oh
long hair long hair
lifts the waves
because drinking oneself high
one wobbles
because of the northwesterly
one shakes
because of wobbling

one remains where one is without moving

because of the dream

one wakes up

because of morals

one moralises

because of the needle

it jabs

because of standing

one doesn't fall

because underneath the lamp

it is dark

because of the sunshine

the eye is dazzled

because the eye is blind

the heart knows

because of presence

one is present

because of absence

one is present

because of the face

one is livid

because of the phone

one calls

because no one answers

one calls in vain

because that's the way it is

it has to be the way

because there's no liquor

one sings

hum gently

no lyrics

rock gently

the sea is tired

the stars are there

the moon is there also

if you don't look up

how can you see?

if you don't look up

you can also see

your heart is drunk

your heart generates wind

the wind comes from the cluster of pores

the wind drowns in the river of veins

because of nihility

there is nothingness

because there is nihility and nothingness

there are things

because there are things

there is nihility and nothingness

because endless

there is end

when you ask why

there is no answer

because because

so, so

ha ha ha ha

I'm dying of happiness

so are you

www.ingramcontent.com/pod-product-compliance
Lightning Source LLC
Chambersburg PA
CBHW021142090426
42740CB00008B/904